The Lamentation

I

Edited by
Philip Brett

HOMAS TALLIS
(c.1505–1585)

© Oxford University Press 1995

OXFORD UNIVERSITY PRESS, MUSIC DEPARTMENT, GREAT CLARENDON STREET, OXFORD OX2 6DP

Printed in Great Britain

The Lamentations of Jeremiah

6

The Lamentations of Jeremiah

The Lamentations of Jeremiah

The Lamentations of Jeremiah

The Lamentations of Jeremiah

The Lamentations of Jeremiah

24

The Lamentations of Jeremiah

The Lamentations of Jeremiah

The Lamentations of Jeremiah

The Lamentations of Jeremiah

The Lamentations of Jeremiah

The Lamentations of Jeremiah

The Lamentations of Jeremiah

The Lamentations of Jeremiah

211

214

The Lamentations of Jeremiah

Reproduced and printed by Halstan & Co. Ltd., Amersham, Bucks., England

TCM 47*b* **The Lamentations of Jeremiah** TALLIS

ISBN 978-0-19-352097-4

9 780193 520974